Mind Your Eyes

Mind Your Eyes

Poems

Marian Frances White

killick press
an imprint of Creative Publishers

St. John's, Newfoundland and Labrador
2003

Le Conseil des Arts | The Canada Council
du Canada | for the Arts

We acknowledge the support of The Canada Council for the Arts for our
publishing program.

We acknowledge the financial support of the Government of Canada through the
Book Publishing Industry Development Program (BPIDP) for our
publishing program.

∞ Printed on acid-free paper

cover art of "The Raven" by Christopher Pratt

Published by
KILLICK PRESS
an imprint of CREATIVE BOOK PUBLISHING
a division of Creative Printers and Publishers Limited
a Print Atlantic associated company
P.O. Box 8660, St. John's, Newfoundland and Labrador A1B 3T7

First Edition
Typeset in 11 point Elegant Garamond

Printed in Canada by:
PRINT ATLANTIC

National Library of Canada Cataloguing in Publication

White, Marian Frances, 1954-
        Mind your eyes / Marian Frances White.

Poems.
ISBN 1-894294-60-2

        I. Title.

PS8595.H4255M55 2003   C811'.54   C2003-904706-7

For Phonse
Eternal Brother
1953 - 2001

**and my poetic father, Terrence White,
who is now with him.**
1917 - 2003

I was looking for someone who had lines in her face
- Cohen

TABLE OF CONTENTS

TRAVEL

Elemental Longing

Lifetime Guarantee in Curley's Cove

We walk over the church hill
turn down toward the brook
stand on the bridge
hands held tight to the rail

a scene with irises
in centre stage is in full view
confident as an actor on opening night
nature concocts
a stellar performance

we poke through a fence
built to keep horses in
make our way through paths
over meadows that offer a lifetime guarantee
for this luxury green carpet

soon the lookout opens to a view
beyond trees to the ocean
where two eagles hold their gaze
collapsed houses dot the cove

down beside *their* beach
stretched across a long flat rock
I know I am not the first woman to lie here
toes dipped in the icy salt water of the North Atlantic

lying here, it's easy to image
the old life lived on the shores of Curley's Cove
fire burned in chimneys
cod fried in cast iron pans
this clothesline once held a wash to be proud of
its impaled stick now dangles a threadbare line

I throw my wet shirt over it
voices call down the shore
rest a spell
mint leaves are picked for tea

ST. MARY'S BAY

Shameless
affectionate gannets
mate by the thousands
webfooted they cling
to ageless granite
hills green with victory
admire their plumage
they have won
a corner of the world
no small wonder

why here
and not the next
ocean-erect cliff
another age-old
question
unanswerable
the sheep *baa*
to the gannet *grrr*
tourists leave
speechless
lens closed
past patches of open iris

ODE TO THE UNITED NAIL FOUNDRY SPECIAL - 1932

She is no Maid of Avalon
gleaming porcelain, chrome and iron
or a Hillcrest shipped from Lunenburg
but cast from townie nails
the UNF stove shines
bountiful, ready to burn

like me she stands aloof
some days cold, other days burning red
ready to blaze even on an August day
or as wind tears in
between bare wood and no gyproc
come winter

what is the difference
baking chanterelle pie in this oven
unlit since the roaring thirties
forged and carved at the nail foundry
a wedding gift, unwrapped
offered to the only woman who fired it up
before me

I call her female
her warmer waiting for toutins*
to comfort an afternoon hunger
I've heard other stories
a woman taking an axe to a stove
that no amount of wood would heat
though golden bread was expected daily
I'll not cook in her, no more,
I hear her curse
until I have a UNF Special

her eyes glow, satisfied
as she boards the St. John's steamer
for Catalina, her hand-picked stove
the foundry's finest
a comfort over the winter
off the Avalon

I stand before her, poised in reverence
split wood in hand, twigs burn
tell me your stories, I whisper,
voices sing
wood crackles

She Got The Berry Hill Woes

There are no blueberries on the hills
to speak of, she says
I mean you can get them
if you walks in far enough
over the marsh and gets down
on your hands and knees
and crawls beneath the trees
I don't mind doing that
for the berries
I forgets everything when I'm pickin'
but the bloody *pickers*, those machines,
got the hills ruined
they shouldn't be allowed
rakes up the white ones with the blue
tears off the leaves; leaves nothin'
to ripen or grow back
I could cry
those *pickers* should be outlawed
and then the berry buyers
pays more for the picker berries
than I can get for the hand-picked ones
don't get me goin' or I'll get the berry picker woes
I got enough wild ones to eat
and some in the freezer for duff* in the winter
so here's your gallon, come back tomorrow
I'll see if there's another bucket-full on the hills
to scrounge
now get on with ya
I got to get back to a game of cards
before they're picked over too

THE UNTOLD STORY

We were a Country, not a colony
when Armine Gosling shouted
"we strive for freedom for ourselves
and for all Newfoundland women"
then May Kennedy jumped from her seat and called:
"to the Country of Newfoundland"

That was before England called us to war
and before the streetcar frightened horses
as they paced along Water St.
their carts full of daily passage
on the waterfront settlers waved
as steamers set sail for Halifax,
London, Boston, New York,
a winter chill did not daunt the resolve
to find another life abroad

Newfoundland was not a joke, it was a proud people
Whiteway, Bond, Squires, even a boy called Joey knew that,
so did Armine, May, Julia, Annie Mitchell and Fannie McNeil
the dailies full of people settling scores
young domestics coming from the Bay*
to find their way up Prescott Street to the grander homes
along Rennies Mill and Circular Rd.
some never made it sailed instead to Boston

What is our history if it buries the past
if it does not tell of Maud Hutchings and Annie White
debate the vote all the way up the Brow
a mantra sounds over the waves —
come back from your maiden voyage
ancient women, shape shifters
to claim our home

HER/E ON THE EDGE

Daylight now is unavailing,
You will come no more,
Call of voice or bell unheeding,
Through life's open door.

From *Doors* by E. J. Pratt, 1932

You were not her/e when I returned
I don't mean at my home
where you never lived
but no longer in this city
in this life that longs for spring
and then for the solstice summer

What does it mean
to drive to Torbay and say
this is the day
her/e on the edge
when I will live no more
no more strength to weave
tales for work companions
smiles for strangers or friends
no more energy to fake
a sashay across the dance floor
to bar hop or bat the ball
to a summer's home run end

But will you remember us
her/e on the edge
harboured beyond your control
does that matter
as long as you have found peace
in a new awakening

FLIP'S WAKE*
MARCH 13, 2000

A cold easterly blew
the day Flip went underground
a good day for dormant leaves
to take flight, released by a sudden thaw

The priest doesn't speak of *Flip*,
lighting magician for every show in town,
but of Gerard's baptism in Christ
doesn't mention the miles of extension chords
hauled to light a show
or of his technical wizardry
but of Jesus and Lazarus
and a grieving Margaret and Mary

We are left with the flight of leaves
wind calls through bare branches
the only technical requirement for this day
is memories:
of Flip Dancing the Goat
of Flip with a Jockey Club Six Pack Crown
all his own
a smile melts to his corner lip
as though a smoke still hung there

Another spirit flies among us
technical artistry
flips the wind
leaves take flight

*For Flip Janes

HEART ATTACK HILL

Tourists think Heart Attack Hill
was nicknamed for the steep ascent
to Gower St. from Duckworth
Nunnery Hill and alleyways jutting the climb
now will it be named after her death
on a wet November afternoon

Marguerite, I sound your name
in case some have already forgotten your battle
in the bustle that continues below us
a man balances a tight rope of barbed wire
pours concrete for a parking garage
where another woman's home used to be

two plastic ribbons strung
around a home mark her life
this is not a celebration of birth
no marker of men gone to war
but of a battle fought daily
on the home front

there is war in the Middle East, in Africa
and war here at home
against women who wash and scrub floors
and can't pay bills, but deliver more children
into a callous world

a war on women who pick their children up
from school and *shush* them quiet
to not disturb the old man
hung over
in the living room

it is a sad day for hearts
and hills
the attack of the soul
when a hill spills a life
and becomes known
for Marguerite's murder

DRIVE-BY SHOOTING

police are over-budget
on reels of yellow tape
a record six murders this year

is there relief in this maze of crime
when a woman's death has been avenged
and a judge says you are charged
with the murder of your brother
face the camera undaunted
no longer afraid for your own life

reflector tape cuts the dusk
brighter than high-beam lights
shot through fog
a white sheet covers
his body in the parking lot
more than a still life
catches rush hour homeward eyes

some call it a drive-by shooting
to warrant a new statistic,
the first for Newfoundland
stories abound, his sister on TV,
bent over, cramped in fear
sleeps with a gun under her pillow
I lived in fear of him, she wails,
many in this city did

the misery of his dead soul
enters dreams where demons
drive him to kill, again and again
dreams of men I see daily
rush down Duckworth St.

Silent K/night Underground

rivers

culverted

to please

city sprawl

trickle

through *man*holes

the cascades

gasp

in the thaw

UNTITLED

She will deliver today
a child or herself
a bundle of packages for thanks
instead of words

She will try one more time
to calm a mind
unsettled in dish water, soup bubbles
she will not drain herself today
down the kitchen sink
or let soup burn
if she gives birth
to herself

Pages of forgotten wishes
a special edition Christmas catalogue
delivered to her door
sale items declare: *your dreams fulfilled*
she would have read it over coffee
if her labour hadn't overwhelmed her
coloured pages burn
the sale on deliverance

AFTER SERVING TIME

his hollow face on the front page
requires a search for human characteristics
his soul unfree to carry lines to eternity

turn the page to national news
west coast pig farms in a blurry focus
and to international news of floods and war with Iraq

turn back to the front page
flashes of life decades ago
clashes with his release from prison

a flood of water blurs the print
but I am not sinking
there is no land slide, no war inside me
just another news story to recycle

WHAT THE FLOWERS SAY

Three distinct flowers bloomed early this summer
hold on even through July
forget-me-nots spread down the rock garden,
devour all soil with their blanket of blue
speak wonders, forget-me-not.

My eye shifts to the bleeding heart
royal in its bleeding, over the stone wall
its stems pump red the centre
on the outside, white, veinlike
only a few lonely hearts dangle
gone is their month of morning glory

Terraced beds bloom purple, white
and now silver dollars bend to the river
where honesty erodes the garden
annuals comfort the fading blooms
impatiens, sparingly cultivated
soon the feverfew will strengthen monkshood tall
to protect black-eyed susans
until the peak of autumn glory

THE BELLS OF IRELAND

I am late planting
the Bells of Ireland
but am I too late
for a white Shamrock bloom
that will root itself
deep seeded
between
Morning Glory
and Poppies
for whom
the Canterbury Bells
toll

This is the Room

This is the room
where I c(r)ave Eavan Boland
her Irish voice a mantra
to the shadow July sun casts
along the bedroom wall
a purple housecoat hangs

Sun shoots through the narrow hallway
down the stairwell to further cast my exit
all the way to Water St.
where the ships dock and predestrians long
for an end to the smell of shame

I take her through streets
as though she were accustomed to this old city
familiar haunts, alleyways,
the Ship Inn and later the Fat Cat
where music fills the night with horns and pipes
old songs, hauntingly new

Are we of the old song, or the new
our voices not stuck in mourning men
gone to sea, our bodies shrill with longing
for we are her/e, Eavan Boland,
Irish women come home

A Sobbing End of August

I called Jennifer the day Diana died
we spoke as if we had known her
beyond paper clippings and news flashings
into the last August night of her life

words slow and catch in our throats
as if she were a long ago friend
now divorced, a single mother
teenage boys

we say we could have done more
as if we had done anything
beyond detailing her anorexia, bulimia,
shy Princess Di, decidedly dead

this wet weekend comforts us
a damp southwest wind keeps many awake
the one night of Diana's life
when the city of lights took her breath away

still life, haunting
more than a paparazzi shot
near Le Tour Eiffel
snapped in time to capture
a sobbing end of August

A New Day Dawns - Epistle

I want to be angry for you today
since I am not your lawyer, your X, mother or lover
just a friend in a west coast daze

I have been following your last romantic day
with him
the late breakfast
long Sunday walk in the park
spring flowers not yet in bloom
later, the drive along the ocean front
winding your way to Cape Spear
where waves crash white as icebergs could
and with more resolve than beaching whales

I picture you on the eastern edge
gazing out over the boardwalk
perhaps thinking this is the closest you have been
to your home country in quite a while
la vie est jolie, you say, très jolie

later that afternoon the car winds back
to catch the sunset over St. John's
your view magnificent from Shea Heights
it is his idea to dine out
this is too perfect a day, you think,
how wonderful to be alive

for privacy sake, I do not imagine
where you eat or what pleases your palate
I know you rarely eat dessert
and that is where we differ

I am not following you like a stalker
nor with an obsession to picture you with him
but to understand the epistle
you later held in your piano-finger hands

I want a divorce, you read
words thrown speechless into the evening dusk
did you sign on the dotted line
before he had time to retract legal jargon
or did he offer living room sonatas
of why he chose to scar a sunset in spring
why not leave the words lying on the table
for you to read after morning yoga asanas
why the details of this new life designed
to perfection without you

I can be angry today
with or without your permission
the ocean still beats tidal waves
here on the pacific island of Galiano
but the ebb and flow is no different
than hearts beating hope,
hope for the new day that dawns
sunrise over the Atlantic

FORBIDDEN ALBA LOVE

You fade
through the departure lounge
like smoke in the wind
I rush to a cigar shop
to purchase a souvenir package
of your favourite cigarettes
Nat Sherman natural smokes since 1935
me, a non-smoker
carry them in a brief case
like data of personal files
at night I open you
enjoy the outlawed scent
let you linger in a ceramic ashtray
beside an open window
you drift into the Halifax night
do not linger in my hotel room
where a housekeeper might report us
forbidden love
on this a smoke-free floor
your scent rests for tonight
on my fingers

How Do I Remember You?

you were not always a clown,
but you made me laugh
you and your lisp whispered truths
between Eastport and Trinity Bight
I especially remember the sunlight
on a field of wild mustard and daisies

you invited me in
as if you were sure I belonged
me, newborn
groping for a place of no fear
I found it there and here, near you

what of this time, this life that unravels
between us? Twenty years too long for many
can it be any less important than when we picked
sea rocket between the silver sand and stone?
its pungent taste unruly as your curly hair

you cannot always comfort me, nor I
find the place in you where chocolate melts cool,
but not solid, perhaps this is the lasting truth in love
that our comfort is our own, for us to know
and share at a moment's notice

tell me now that we will live happily ever after
and I will know you are lying, tell me we will search
for a life full of distant and tangible cravings
and I will know this love is etched into the season
where iris bloom and wild roses smell so sweet
we will think we are once again in the south of France
our daughter dipping her toes in the Riviera
there is a place between the face of two people
that no one else can tread

A Tincture of Remember Now

You have left me a taste of German chocolate
to sweeten this August dawn
and a lingering desire from your mouth
to paint me in my foolish chefs' hat
frying spelt pancakes
to serve with wild blueberries
add a dribble of Quebec maple syrup
(a gift from your vacation in the Eastern Townships)

On this page I squeeze words
beside the list you and I made
of things we wanted to do with each other
visit the artist colony on Bell Island
pack a picnic basket to fill a day walking over Flatrock
hear music under a dark sky at Cape Spear
follow the whales out
pass the puffin sanctuary in Witles Bay

Yes, you have left me
with a brush stroke of the iris stem
and words to lick away the onion memory
unheard of solace on this exposed rock
we return to words painted on the page
and I will tell you how the *Matthew* sailed
unceremoniously out the St. John's Harbour
while you flew deep into another continent
your Canadian accent intact

And when will the solstice sun
draw us back to the swimming hole
where a mellow waterfall released our backs free
the smell of the forest undergrowth
begs us to distill a tincture
of remember now

Mashes Folly

THE PERSONA OF MASHES FOLLY

Mashes Folly is where I nearly went
over the Perry's Cove cliff in a storm
saved by the bells on the horse and sleigh
that brought me back to the road
I fell through the door
into Florence's arms
at four a.m.

I don't ever want to relive that night
at eighty-six father goes white
every time he tells us
shakes his head, continues
and the very next day
I had to boat back to Bell Island
it's not very often
I felt like punching a man
but I had to hold back my hand
when the boss accused me
of going overboard
drinking beer all weekend

I never drank back then
and even if I did
the sound of the sea
below the cliff
well, it kept me
sober as a judge

THE GOLD RUSH

We listen
like attentive children
as father retells the story
of how grandma rose up the canvas
and tucked a letter underneath
from her brother Jim
and that's where it stayed
until the house was torn down
taken wall by wall
to its new home up the shore

father, a mere lad,
didn't question the letter
estate, gold rush, claim inheritance
from his Uncle Jim Sloan
who went to Alaska
during the Boer War
and never returned
to Perry's Cove

I've opened an account for you,
the letter read,
but what good was an account
the fishing bank
off the north shore
that's all we knew

NECESSARY SECRETS

During the war
mother and father married
father had four dollars in his pocket
gave mother two
kept the other two for train passage
and living expenses at his boarding house
on George St. in St. John's
mother was left to the wind of memory
looking to the sea for answers
to dreams she could feel, but not imagine

I wasn't born until seven voices later
shook her awake to children
crying for toast and morning black tea
those early years
she waited for him to return
though he could not share stories
of secret work on the southside hills
in an ammunition factory

mother spoke of how her life was invaded
by wind and goats paths and only one radio
in the corner cove called White's Room
picture summers there:
perked ears outside the open window
the sea beyond and a dozen ears listen over the air waves
for what she wants to hear: Ted is coming home
watch for the train from St. John's, through Avondale to Carbonear
then for the buggy ride over the hills to Perry's Cove

picture mother walking
as she told me she often did
not to a clear pond to swim
but to endless footpaths made by women

who longed for their husbands' return
from war work in the city

an evening chill
came up over the Bay
made her wish she had a sweater
the wind shifts south
his familiar face cuts through the fog
more real than imagined

An Eye To The Storm

Father did not get home
for Christmas
the winter you were born
saved his time off for a February birthing
but mother took in a January storm
the same day she made flannel nightdresses
for both of you

in a storm that fought
like a knight in armour
their Newfoundland pony made it
through the snow drifts
all the way to Carbonear
from Perry's Cove
where a doctor sat on the icy sleigh
recalling the comfort of his fireplace
as he drove with Uncle Moss
to White's Room

Mother was left with a beach rock at her feet
warmed on the stove that fed them
the oil lamp followed his shadow
past the stove, up the narrow stairs
to her January bed
the wail of the wind competed with hers
the weight of patched worked quilts
kept her from shaking

all night father dreamed
of his week off work to be there
in place of the beach rock
and grandma breathed deep breaths
to steam the window clear
enough to have an eye to the storm

then you were born
and a telegram sent in the calm after the storm
read: *Florence and baby are fine*
that was the winter Christmas came late
and you came early

No Present Without the Past

wood is stored
where an outhouse once stood
indelibly defined
i walk around its aura
otherwise fears fall into shadows

down over
dwarf concrete steps
iris bulge purple
beyond springtime

can the gooseberry bush still produce berries
thousands squat between fingers and squirt
into each other's mouths, bitter
we would bathe beneath the trellis
in the summer Sunday sun

dinner eaten. dishes washed.
no extra chores on Sunday.
memories dizzy these minuscule steps
around the corner bleeding hearts bloom
to celebrate, no present without the past

Eighty Year Old Woman Hauls Slabs of Wood

The fog has lifted
we can see out the bay
wanna go for a drive, just for an hour, I plea
a drive - after lunch - she scolds,
and me with no work done yet today

I point past the kitchen window
clothes hang uniformly on the line,
to the spotless floor,
to dinner plates washed, drip drying
I suppose we can, she concedes,
we'll take your father's truck

Up the Bay, we drive down back roads
and talk of lives gone, homes boarded up
lace curtains, threadbare in windows
chimneys missing bricks
bottomless boats in decaying heaps of hay

Further along mother eyes a mound of wood pallets
stacked beside an abandoned fish meal plant
they're good slabs for kindling, she says,
if Ted were with me we'd stop for a load
I suppose that's too much for you,
you with your good clothes on

This is her challenge

I gear down, turn around
drive through the gate marked:
>   *Private Wharf:*
>   *No Unauthorized Vehicles*
>   *Beyond This Point*

Drive on through, she indicates with her finger
straight ahead, never mind the sign
no one will bother us
and she's right, no one does

The pallets are heavy after winter and two days rain
she lifts each with certainty
I follow her rhythm, avoid tripping and nails,
until the truck is filled to capacity
a long, knotted rope secures the load

Driving down the Bay road
she sees me glance in the mirror
you needn't worry about that load holdin'
Ted usually has it blocked up to the roof of the cab
you're lucky, we got away with a small load

Drive up the back lane, she suggests,
children will soon be out of school
I back the truck to the high point of land
beyond *his* driveway and *her* flower garden
the earth is soft, wheels dig in
we'll have to unload it from here, she says undaunted
an hour later, pleased with the effort, we go inside

Mother adds wood to the fire, boils the kettle, pours tea
if you weren't going back to town, she says
as she spreads bakeapple jam over homemade bread
I'd say to go for another load
but I know you got some poetry thing to attend
my, it's a fine day now, the sky is clearing
I hate to think of all that wood lying up there, rotting
....don't get me wrong,
I know a second load would be too much on you

This is her second challenge

We finish tea and the last heel of bread
get back in the cab
this time with proper clothes for the task
rubberized gloves and thick-soled boots
as tough as nails

A young woman walks her dog down the lane
stops to inquire about father in hospital
eighty looks good on you, she says
what are you doing with yourself these days
mother folds her feet to hide work boots,
nothing much, making lots of jam, she waves good-bye
I hope we don't meet her on the way back, she sputters,
I can hide the boots, but not a fine load of slabs

This time we load wood high to the level of the cab
knot the rope secure for the return ride
this time I drive pass the driveway and flower bed
find the rhythm to unload her slabs

I love doing this, she says,
this isn't work, it's pleasure
the fresh air, the exercise
why did you say you were going back to town?

A women's poetry reading
March 8th every year

Sure wood is a poem, she laughs,
you can call this one
eighty year old woman
hauls a load of wood *or*
she's as tough as nails, and be sure to say
there's a line in every slab

QUEEN MOTHER

Mother whispers prayers
into the Bonavista night
a wise owl, she whistles Hail Mary's
her meditation for sleep
no helicopter escorted m/ot/her here
but I, her daughter-in-waiting
tuck sheets to her chin and listen
to prayers whispered in the calm
of this sacred night

no room at the town inn,
we wake to the early morning bark
of a house dog and hungry cry of gulls
anxious to hear toast and tea commentary
of the Queen Mother and her entourage
flying in to wave us
five-hundred-year-old
colonized greetings

Jacob's Hands

Jacob's hands stretch into the night
air pans between his one-inch fingers
he fists away the spirits
that disturb his sleep

As if in prayer
his fingers rise and join each other
oh holy night, he gives thanks
for warm milk that greets his throat

Sucking sounds continue
until lips release the nipple
fingers fly one last time to grip the night air
and then, oh so gently, they fall to his side
Jacob is asleep.

The Longest Winter Ever

Jacob's four, he says
this snow is forever
I thought it was only to slide on
I don't want snow to be forever
I want the grass
I miss green

snow touches the clouds
flips over Nan's house
where are the flowers she planted
we didn't pick all of them
I didn't mean to: his bottom lip turns up

I want to go to the beach
where is the sand
how can the birds feed
where are the ducks
tell the wind to stop
just for a second

you said it is spring
but I want leaves on trees
and the sun warm so I don't need a coat
my boots are tired of lifting my feet
when can I kick them off
to play in the park

No, I don't want to make
another snow creature
this is *hor-ri-ble*
Jacob kicks snow from the step
you're not coming inside with us
no, not now snow
not ever

THE EMPTY HUBBARD
OCTOBER 1996

Aunt Cecily gave herself up to death
called for her daughters, and the priest
on a quiet Thursday morning
when adults work and children study at school

gone is her bloated form
tired of medication and saying
I'm sorry to the nurses
who wipe away her jello meals

a plastic ivory casket, chosen long ago
matches her non-discerning taste
as if the earth craved
frivolity

we all cried
as the ivory lowered her from view
sisters, brother, daughter, sons, nieces, nephews
who ate from her hubbard
like a fairy pantry, food poured onto the table
a spread of bread and jam, fruit cocktail with Nestle's cream
generous offerings after a Sunday drive over the marsh
these memories she leaves each of us
standing here, hungry for more

SURVIVAL TIN BOX

stored in the root cellar
in a square biscuit box
with a winter's tale:

1 lb. green lentils
2 lbs. brown rice
1 lb. basmati white long grain
1 lb. split peas
2 lbs. red lentils
2 oz. mixed dried herbs with vegetables
6 oz. vegetable broth and seasoning

and a prayer:
may the rodents
need to gnaw on this
long before me

No Name Ice Cream

Sheilagh's Brush* evokes
a flash of ice cream memory
a brick, a barrel, or a tub, brings me back
to Mavis and her mother's corner store

Mrs. Shortfoot sold three flavours
vanilla, chocolate, neapolitan
with my index finger I scrape
the bottom of the barrel
a treat, had Mavis not told me her mother was too cheap
to give us a real ice cream in a sugar cone

I savour every lick
even as wax melts
with the neapolitan cream, assure myself
the empty barrel could have been offered
like a sacred host to another drooling child

memory of taste evokes pleasure
and something close to shame
.... now the forty year old memory fails me
I wade knee-deep into a freak snow storm
comforted by the wail of Sheilagh's Brush

VAN GOGH

I am a Van Gogh today
ear bandaged
sound impaired
sipping tea
to a December wail

slowly I rise upright
still, the room spins
as if Marianne Faithful
was here singing loud
about Lucy Jordan

no paint brush to airmark a moment
no sketch of sunflowers swaying
outside this hospital window
a silent pen etches words
along a static line

internal noise
comforted by past lives
and the wind outside
deliberate, whispers
you are not forgotten
Van Gogh

ANAÏS NIN

Anais Nin is dead
sweat on sheets
the only Sunday morning
comfort

but what is this small body doing
her/e al/one
as though there were no one
in need of blueberry bagels
and raspberry tea

there is a cave between wor(l)ds
this blank p/age and pen
a place that hides meaning and
makes room for essential longing
but where the breeze to cool armpits
who to whisper slow, slow
death comes to love
all too final

WHAT DREAMS BECOME

What is it I see here
in this shrine of God
mother stands beside me
whispering Amen, in time
with the congregation

stations of the cross I examine
no longer lost in the agony Jesus suffered
but observe the craft and skill to recreate
the illusion of pain
time to contemplate the physical challenge
to bring marble statues from Spain
to this island, vesseled in high seas
hung in the order of denial and reverence
I gaze toward Jesus, nailed to the cross
Lent will soon shroud his agony from view

I am not here with school girls on a mission
though I recognize faces in pews
full of familiar creaking sounds
a faint cough grows and swells
through the echo of hymns
age has changed her features
but not the cough, identifiable
only here do I remember her husband died
while shopping for school shoes with their daughter
another man gently pats her back,
a comfort even to me

church pews have been removed
red carpet rolled out to make way for a wheelchair
the priest stops to pat a boy's head
a long ago classmate wheels her son
to the communion altar

saintly, a tall figure files by
a daughter with the same slender features, follows her
never have I experienced this communion of saints
Sunday is altered perpetually

Day two
shopping, banking with mother
(after Monday morning clothes washing, of course)
a face pulls me back
across the desk sits a memory, now a manager
of mother's life savings
in her eyes we are teens
trying to solve Monday's math problems

small talk and name pins tell stories
of no companion, no children of her own
my emblem, a pocket-size graduation photo
you never came to yours, she reminds me,
we called you a zealot back then

the bank takes good care of its own, she smiles
my girlfriends and I take a two week vacation
in the Caribbean, every two years, she adds
keying in personal data

lines part between teenage fantasy and adult reality
did we ever think, back then,
what dreams become
sign here, she points,
never mind what we were taught
no need to read the fine print
above the line

MIND YOUR EYES

Memory One:
Phonse and me at the carnival
on a Ferris wheel
me shit baked, legs dangle from the top
him laughin', *mind your eyes*, he screams
shakin' the seat, fierce and fearless

Memory Two:
the narrow lane
ends at the bottom of church hill
where go-carts raced
I was sure Phonse would win
had watched the seventh child, age seven
saw and hammer and nail the seat that would land him
very near where the dream took me

but where are you now
speeding past this realm of understanding
gliding without tinted glasses
to guarantee first-place position

mind your eyes, you call
not tight to the wheel made from our sister's baby carriage
but to the glow spotlighting the dream of the rocky lane

Memory Three:
he flicks the switch
mind your eyes or the lamp will blind you
pull the patchwork blanket to your brow
soft, dark, cool, everything bathed in white
you now move toward
the shocking truth of death is light
and then life ever after
illuminates childhood dreams

Travel

Friday Night, Jamaican Style

Reggae music blares
through the streets
of Mo Bay
deep
into a revival meeting
in the heart of Negril
Praise the Lord
Repent or Perish
the preacher shouts
even I do not object
for praise comes easy
bound between
sliced pineapple
scented white witch tales
curved between
Ting juice stands and
grotto slave lives long lived
not long enough gone
but we are here
to witness the coral shores
edging white
against black feet
a translucent blue green ocean
the moonlight glorifies
we sink
deeper into the heart
of a Friday night
Jamaican style

BLUE MOUNTAIN COFFEE

Blue Mountain will sit here
calm in the face of hurricane or drought
uncensored by the season that
pushes banana trees tall and
mango branches broad-leafed
their fruit hurries to ripen and fall
into our hands

At night
fireflies guard these mountains
made tame by lack of longing
for stars to torch the horizon
and fall between the gorge
gurgling deep below

There is life I will never see
cave driven
blended so finely with the green
that the dark of this night
is one with the day
mysterious Jamaica, coffee grinds
an elemental sounding

MAMMEE BAY STONES

I have left Timothy Findley
on the night table
in a hut
beside this tropical ocean
where waves
roar and wash
over his words
like *Stones*
sun will later curl
the edges
rough
as though real life
were textured
leaves fall
to the cove
below Mammee Bay
fall
not crisp
after an autumn chill
off the Atlantic
but flaky
dried in the Jamaican sun

perhaps Findley
touched by the ocean
will offer retribution
distance
hopes to bring

CARIBBEAN WAVE

I remind myself
this is a Caribbean wave
at midnight in St. Anne's Bay
where the night has no rhythm
even as Reggae beats
into the heat of Saturday night

to be here in April
fools fall face first
into the pool
who will question
the church service
black as night
mysterious and beautiful
with the next Caribbean wave
I dive in

In Black and White

Sunbathers stretch city limbs
across lounge chairs
while a black man rakes
seaweed that might fall
between vacationers' toes
a child cries behind me
not a black child where a dark momma
cuddles him breast deep
his mother dances with her lover
in the waves

This is beach party night on the resort
a parade of waiters design the table
while Ja cooks, in their white hats,
attend the grill and much, much more
tourists take a pre-dinner siesta
shower away tropical sweat
powder dry, change into evening silk

outside torches are lit, time
neither advances, nor do we lose an hour
it remains as when slaves escaped
through the Grotto Caves
is this the resort where they landed
to eat jerk chicken or curried goat
with heart of palm in vinegarette
ending with coconut angel food cake
where are the black angels to carry exhausted
waiters, tired from serving rum
or lighting Cuban cigars and listening
to how hard businessmen work back in Ohio
it's a starry, starry night behind the grill
I sit here, camera in hand to capture the contrast

On Visiting Mary Pratt's Studio

Mary Pratt was eighteen in 1954, the year I was born.
in her studio, she shows guests a watercolor from that year
here, she says, I am not trying to accomplish anything
or do anything right, just paint an impression of what I see.
Trying to do things right came later.

Upstairs my eye catches a Christopher Pratt
outport scene; two houses, blue tones in the background
foreground white sheets blowing in the wind
and a raven, a large single raven soars by
a cover of a book
the challenge: to write one worthy of the raven's gaze
quicker than a brush stroke
I turn to Mary's canvas
before her guests eye my torment
that seems the right thing to do.

TINY SHRINES

tiny shrines
daunt the coastline to Sithonia
its arm stretches
over the Halkidiki Peninsula
what woman stood in this doorway
not to snap a memory shot of Greece
but to pray
as does a mother in Pouch Cove
that her son will return
from a day on the sea

the smell of beeswax permeates the air
over-powering olive trees of the region
one candle is lit for all I know
and do not know
press tiny discards
the castaways
into a side pocket

this is the souvenir
to take back home

WHERE THE THESSALONIKIANS REST

parched earth
windswept gardens
birds chirp
an eternal message
this is the destiny
of the *Illiad of Homer*
hot, noisy, plentiful
kids swing
as the Aegean Sea
rolls on

FUGITIVE PIECES CONTINUES

The sparkle on the Aegean Sea
never dulls in the sunlight
olives press liquid in mouth
melt soft with chick pea bread
exotic taste once unknown in the new world
here on the Halkidiki Peninsula
German tourists order more than Heinken

dance for us, they shout, we are on holidays
the Greek god waiters oblige
video cameras capture the moment
a few duck behind pillars
now we will laugh, I think I hear them say,
for what do I know, but a few words of German
everything else is Greek to me

we leave the dinner table
where Makedonikos regional red wine pours freely
but it's the Rapsani white Germans admire
with breaded fish, glasses ting to fill a place
where no table talk can be exchanged

I turn back to see if tourists joined the Greek gods
in a frolic around the dance floor
in the centre of the Macedonian sun
painted with pride on marble
for all to walk on, or strut across

Atos has other plans for this Byzantine journey
Fugitive Pieces snatched off a bookshelf
Michaels' tale takes me into dreams of German camps
where soldiers eat curried goat and make merry
while native Greeks starve, naked,
huddled in the night

awake I hear voices in the courtyard
not screaming orders, but teasing one another
to jump into the pool
after all it is also their last night of vacation
merciful they stumble in a stupor
on their knees they pray to end the night
with the blessings of Aphrodite upon them

fitful I drift back into ancient dreams
bound by bed and wrought iron balcony
that shakes with German laughter
I quote them passages from Anne Michaels
then they offer me baklava, chocolate dipped oranges
ozo water

parched, I wake late
rush to catch the flight from Thessaloniki to Münich
dreams prepare the soul for travel beyond borders
later, on the flight to Toronto, I pray
for the free spirit of Atos and Jakob
to fly home with me

Münich Tastes Spring

A bright, blue, spring sky
spreads over Münich
Mirabelle trees blossom off Twyla's balcony
the aroma of East Indian cuisine rises up

a woman hangs her wash in the courtyard
another carries her basket to market
an ordinary day in a startling city
where there is cause to make daily life common

calm descends, cleanliness ordered,
order does not come naturally
to a million-plus Volk
no obelisk to the third reich
no souvenirs of a time not long enough gone
but beer steins and alpine hats
to typify the new Germany

we savour Barlauch
spread over yellow roasted potatoes and
steamed Jerusalem artichokes
a taste as wild as the garlic that names it
drink in the spicy air
with a side pickle in our teeth
admire the German city decor
an unblemished face lift

bells toll
birds chirp prayers
for all who have not survived
to admire a bright blue spring sky
spread over Münich

Million Dollar Tip

I was pissed
not from a night on the town
but from missing the conference shuttle
back to Mississauga, a city of pallid pulse

how much you wanna pay
a thick- throated cabbie
lowers his snowy window onto Yonge St.
twenty bucks, I offer
it'll cost you thirty to go way the hell out pass the airport
that's a steal, he adds and raises his window tight to my nose
there goes my per diem, I mumble
and help myself to the back seat

Then he starts in, where you from
Newfoundland, I say,
never been there, but my wife and I have a dream
when we retire, we want to escape this city and drive
from one end of the Country to the other
why go to the Alps when you have the Rockies
I hear you make a mean meal of fish and chips on the Rock

I get so fed up with complainers, he snarls,
came here in the 70s with my suitcase half full
thirty-five dollars in my pocket
only half my boat fare paid
been driving a cab ever since
paid the other half back that first year
met a great woman, raised two kids. Not like me.
They have a good education. Speak French.
Can work anywhere in this Country.
I tell them, whatever you do, like it.
that's the answer to being happy

Whata ya think of Quebec?
you know what, I wish I had it so good
whata Country, French on everything
not like in my old world, Greece
haven't been back since I escaped the chaos of Athens
my kids will visit, but me,
this is my home, Canada. I love this Country
you know what I think?
I think Quebecers secretly love it here too
you don't see too many of them running home to Greece

I glance through the back window at the blowing snow
an escape to Greece seems a viable option
just when I think he is oblivious to my island fantasy he adds:
now a vacation there would be welcome,
especially for you from Newfoundland,
pretty cold down there, but I hear
you got some hot-headed politicians
who could melt icebergs
we got more in common than you think
all that blue ocean against the white ice
he points to the Greek flag glued to his dash
and a maple leaf taped beside it
after all, home is where the heart is

Gees, here's your hotel already
the ride wasn't that long after all
give me a twenty, that'll do
what's this, your business card
ah Canadians, that's worth a million dollar tip
got an envelope full, my wife and I
you wait and see, we'll drop by in a few years
when we escape this city and
take that dream trip down east

NO WARNING

It is not your average May Day
on Boulevard St. Jean
a bus shelter blocks a north wind
while I wait for the metro connection to centreville

The wait is not tiresome
I crack the cover of *the whole woman*,
Germaine Greer promised
sixties feminists would appreciate

L'autobus est en retard, a sixty-something woman remarks
the second she crosses the boulevard to enter the bus shelter
Pas encore, I offer and lower my eyes to page one:
> "This sequel to *The Female Eunuch* is the book
> I said I would never write."

A siren blares past the shelter, both of us shift and ignore it

She switches to English, (perhaps thinking this was why
I offered limited conversation)
Do you ever think that today might be the end of the world?
I glance to my left, no one has arrived,
the question dangles in the air
such a sobering querry, after a massage,
on the first day of my holiday in Montreal

Oui, I say, but not today.

Ma mère, she continues, was eighty-nine short two weeks
when she died last winter
but *pensez-vous* how strange life is, how unpredictable?

I want to escape the plastic hut, no longer a shelter
but answer, *ah oui, la vie est bizarre*

ma fille died last year, she continues, age thirty-three
left three children to return to her ex-husband
they now live on a military base in Halifax
why would God take *ma fille* and keep *ma mère* here?
Martha was all there for her *petite filles*
No warning, she died over a weekend of a brain aneurism
Des jours, I think we are born with a destiny, *pensez-vous*?

I close Greer on her sentence:
"It's time to get angry again",
stand up to face her and say
I'm sorry to hear all this

Oh, you're not very tall, *vous êtes petite*, she says out loud,
you look a lot taller sitting down.
I guess your mother taught you to stand tall.
(images of nuns in long black veils, yard sticks comes to mind
but I keep this image to myself, she has enough on her mind)
Who will teach my grandchildren to sit tall? she asks

Il fait froid en mai, I turn to the weather for light conversation
she continues, *des enfants* have ways to cope with misfortune
my granddaughter tells me that it is her mother, not her father,
who now lives very far away,
and she can only visit when we go to her gravesite *en été*.
C'est dur, la vie est dur, n'est-ce pas?

Je ne sais pas pourquoi I'm telling you all this
You from Montreal?
No, Terre-Neuve.
Oh, where we get our hydro power
that's a sore point, she says, we won't talk about sore points
the real power is on the street

a man walks down the boulevard and spits
in the 50s you would be arrested for that, she scolds,
spitting, I mean, with TB everywhere

perhaps I have found a way to conversation with her, I say,
my father had tuberculous, he lived in a sanatorium
the entire first year of my life
mother dropped me on the bed
when she saw him walk up the lane
his suitcase in one hand
a package for us in the other

but now she is running from my story
ah, voila, l'autobus arrive
don't talk to strangers, I tell my grandchildren
that's the biggest lesson I can teach them
she steps onto the bus
bon vacances

WHAT IS NOT NEGOTIABLE
FOR GERRY ROGERS

I did not know you here
where the wind and rain
could mask a longing

somewhere between rue St. Laurent
and L'Esplanade we met
to choose ripe mangos for breakfast
you the champion bargain hunter

what I remember now are the birds
frantic outside the room
where you sheltered me
calm after an August rain

and always the struggle
the search for words
that would eradicate
fear

extreme voices sound
identical with survival
that came by salsa dancing the night away
and now, you, here, not so far away

me, how lucky
you once said
truth is not negotiable

COLD CURRENCY

I remember these cobblestone streets
the uneven footpath through Central Station
and up Pearl St.
I remember the flower stand where
no fresh stems were purchased, not once.
I remember more the lilac in bloom
outside the bedroom window
its scent battled Boston Harbour for survival

footprints leave no trail on cobblestones
hollow, incessant sounds
echo the pedestrian pace
between two bricks lies a penny
my mother would say:
find a penny, have luck all day
pass it on, your luck is sure to stay

but here on Cambridge St.
unsure of my luck
I clinch the Lincoln penny
as though it were an airline ticket
back to Canada

I remember too, Filenes
not the posh store in Central Square
but the bargain basement, nestled in Quincy Market
you brought me an elegant bathrobe
ten dollars, such luxury

I do not remember lounging in it all day
but the possibility of doing just that filled me
mostly I remember
my belly swelling into July

Some nights are the same as then
someone else lives (and hopefully loves)
in the second floor back room on Pearl St.
another illegal alien glues taps to shoes
in a back alley factory
graffitied with *nos venceremos*
acrid odours cling to foreign souls
daily commuters shut down in the subway

Boston smells the same, yet novel
every subway station has a flower stand
carnation, lily and rose stems sell for pennies
but would I ever again walk barefoot on Newbury
I drive through Boston Common
en route to Jamaica Plain
pass Paul Revere as he rides to a tea party
cold currency, warm memories

On Pretending to be a Harvard Student

Really, I'm just taking a detour
from the revival in Harvard Square
bass and violin students strum for change
while a freshman tour of Harvard University
begins and I slip into
the story of the three books carved
beside the statue of Professor Harvard
two that symbolize textbook learning and one
closed book to illustrate non-academic discovery
Harvard is for everyone, so the guide says
I could be his mother, but I can't tell his story

Later we all stand on the steps
of the Harry Widener Library
no one notices me shift out of place
we listen to the tale of Widener, the student,
who drowned when the *Titanic* sank
his mother gave money to build this library
with the stipulation all Harvard students
learn to swim before graduating

I want to interrupt, to say the *Titanic* sank
close to the shores of my home
perhaps he still lies in his watery Newfoundland grave
but by now the guide is telling us
Harry was found and buried in Boston Common

I break off from the tour
like a student skipping class
it's the Schlesinger Library I need
the one near Radcliff Hall
where the stories of women
are told with equal gallantry

Really, I'm just pretending to be a Harvard student
I sit on the grass, like dozens of book worms around me
but neither Eavan Boland or May Kennedy
are on this course of study
a sudden wind pulls this page
from under the tree that hovers over me
out through the Harvard gates I run
to catch up with my gaze

Day two, I'm back
Japanese tourists snap photos of the arch
that enters Cambridge St.
the stained glass in the hallway of the medical school
is a favourite tourist shot
but I am a student today, on too tight a budget
to take photographs
for a walk down memory lane
I stroll to the corner café
where a Harvard student washes dishes
another sells fresh cut roses
further down the square
I stop
edge myself closer
to relive a craving
unfathomable

SEATTLE DAWN

the stairs of College Inn
are easier to climb with the warm taste of Rioja
slurping between teeth
there is a poem in Seattle
tucked in between Afgan taxi drivers
who talk on the benefits of chewing raw rice
and a Jamaican beat on 45th and University

some nights, like this, I hesitate
to brush away the taste of pecan pie
crunched in between the Rioja.
the mayor of Seattle, in his welcome address to poets
says he takes great pride in the ethnic diversity of his people

but I am thrown back to Irishtown
and the roots of longing
stems of lavender and columbine cheer me
as the night merges time zones
workers set their morning prayer
to Mount Rainier eruptions
I recite Denise Levertov (1923-1997):
a poem is a form of prayer
and leave Seattle to its dawn

THE THREE SISTERS

Majestic
sulfur mountains
formidable
snow-capped
in June sun
only the gondola
dares
traverse
the edges
of Banff

below
film dealers
play out
their song and dance
vying
for the chance
to beat the deal
three sisters
have made
in perpetuity
with each other

STREET PAINTERS

paintings dance
with the flick of a brush
seamless stream of clourful people
stroll down the Champs d'Élysées
while a steady stream of deux chevals
circle l'Arc de Triumph
Napoleon knew he was building
a monument the world would admire

Nijinsky rests in Montmartre
Simone de Beauvoir took herself out
to breakfast along Rue de la Gaité
Jean-Paul awaites her return from a tryst
at la Coupole where Josephine Baker danced
on the corner of St. Michel and St. Germain
Nureyev exiled himself to a life on point

perspective everything in this city of lights
where street painters interpret millions
with the flick of their brush

A WINTER IN MAJORCA

*A Winter In Majorca** you wrote 1838 to 1839
purchased today in one of Palma's souvenir shops for 975 pesatas
tucked in among the ceramic tile, clay earthenware pots and
biblical mementos

you walked through Palma with your children, and these pages
along this rock smooth street you found
refuge from the Paris winter

outside Café Riolta, a woman and her two children stroll
a flow of gutturals between them
as they torment and love each other

I hear you call to your children to keep up with your pace
not the Majorcan flare, but the Parisienne
step out for a promenade along the canal

December 15, 1838 you arrived in war-torn Palma
Barcelona now leagues away from here
made your way by horse and carriage over these virgin
treacherous hills
you, a lady not in waiting
war troubled Majorcans, even then you feared nothing
but the lasting sadness of war itself

Could you hear Chopin's piano echo
through the monastery wall?
your valor still intact after the winding climb
Chopin too weak to greet you as I do now
I brave the cliffs of Soller
dusk falls around your words printed here in Valledemosa
the books of George Sand, as you call them,
children born of the same mother

Notes and Acknowledgements

The author wishes to thank the Newfoundland and Labrador Arts Council and the City of St. John's for its financial support. Extra special thanks to Beni Malone for his sharp and caring eye.

* toutins or toutons are fried bread dough.
* duff: a boiled pudding made with fresh berries.
* Bay is the name for an outport coastal settlement in Newfoundland.
* a freak snowstorm that occurs around St. Paddy's Day, March 17th, also known as the Equinox Gale.